W9-AMQ-621

Amazing Animal Architects

AMAZING
Animal Architects
of the Air

A 4D BOOK

by Mari Schuh

Consultants:
James L. Gould
Professor
Department of Ecology and Evolutionary Biology
Princeton University

Carol Grant Gould
Science Writer
Princeton, N.J.

PEBBLE
a capstone imprint

First Facts are published by Pebble
1710 Roe Crest Drive, North Mankato, Minnesota 56003
www.mycapstone.com

Library of Congress Cataloging-in-Publication Data
Names: Schuh, Mari C., 1975- author.
Title: Amazing animal architects of the air : A 4D book / by Mari Schuh.
Description: North Mankato, Minnesota : an imprint of Pebble, [2019] |
   Series: First facts. Amazing animal architects | Audience: Ages 6–8. |
   Includes index.
Identifiers: LCCN 2017057832 (print) | LCCN 2018000323 (ebook) | ISBN
   9781543526905 (ebook PDF) | ISBN 9781543526820 (hardcover) | ISBN
   9781543526868 (pbk.)
Subjects: LCSH: Nests—Juvenile literature. | Animals—Habitations—Juvenile
   literature. | Animal behavior—Juvenile literature.
Classification: LCC QL676.2 (ebook) | LCC QL676.2 .S38385 2018 (print) | DDC
   591.56/4—dc23
LC record available at https://lccn.loc.gov/2017057832

Editorial Credits
Karen Aleo, editor; Sarah Bennett, designer; Morgan Walters, media researcher;
Tori Abraham, production specialist

Photo Credits
Alamy: Premaphotos, 15; Dreamstime: Karoline Cullen, 9; Minden Pictures: Tony Heald, 7;
Shutterstock: Chutima Chaochaiya, (blueprint) design element, CRS PHOTO, 17, Janos Rautonen,
13, Kristel Segeren, 11, Miloje, (grunge) design element, Natalia5988, (brush grunge) design
element, Peter Hermes Furian, (map) design element, S.R. Maglione, Cover, Vishnevskiy Vasily, 5,
19, Wang LiQiang, 10; SuperStock: Biosphoto, 21

Printed in China.
000306

Table of Contents

Home Sweet Home

High in the trees, animals are busy building their nests. Leaves, sticks, and mud help them build their homes. These nests keep the animals and their **offspring** safe. Animals build their homes in some amazing ways.

offspring—the young of a person, animal, or plant

A shrike sits on its nest.

Red Ovenbirds

Red ovenbirds mix mud and grass to make their **domed** nests. The nests have a side entrance. This entrance makes the nests look like small ovens. The birds also build a curved wall inside their homes. It makes a safe area for their eggs. **Predators** can't see or reach the eggs behind the wall.

FACT

Red ovenbirds make an opening at the top of the curved wall. They can squeeze through this opening to take care of their eggs.

domed—rounded on top
predator—an animal that hunts other animals for food

Ovenbird nests are found on fence posts, roof ledges, and tree branches.

RANGE MAP

7

Bald Eagles

Bald eagles live up high in tall trees. A male and female build a huge nest made of sticks. They build their nests in layers. Grass, feathers, and plant stems make a soft center. The big nest is strong enough to hold the growing family inside. The nest grows as the adult pair adds more sticks every year.

FACT

Bald eagles build some of the biggest bird nests in the world. Their nests can be 5 to 6 feet (1.5 to 1.8 meters) wide and 2 to 4 feet (0.6 to 1.2 meters) tall!

WHERE BALD EAGLES LIVE

Look up in the tallest trees near rivers and lakes. Bald eagle nests are near water, so they can hunt for fish.

RANGE MAP

Montezuma Oropendolas

Near the Caribbean Sea, gold-tailed birds make hanging nests in rain forest trees. These nests look like drooping sacks. The long nests keep eggs from falling out when the wind blows.

Females **weave** the nests on tall trees that are away from other trees. Then monkeys and other predators can't grab the eggs.

pronunciation: Montezuma oropendola
(mohn-teh-ZOO-ma or-oh-PEN-do-la)

weave—to pass grass, sticks, and other materials over and under one another to make a nest

Montezuma oropendolas build nests in large trees that are not near other trees.

FACT

More than 100 nests can hang from one tree.

Sociable Weavers

Hundreds of **sociable** weavers share a tree nest that looks like a haystack. Just one nest can have more than a hundred chambers. A bird pair lives in each chamber.

The birds use sticks to make a roof that keeps out rain and the sun. Soft grass and fur fill the chambers. Spiky straw is used for the entrances to keep out snakes.

sociable—tending to live in groups or packs

Sociable weavers build in trees with long trunks and high branches. These trees make it hard for predators to reach the nest.

RANGE MAP

Weaver Ants

Weaver ants use **silk** from ant **larvae** to make their leafy nests. The ants grab leaves with their jaws and feet. Then they pull leaves together.

Other ants gather larvae from the old nest. They squeeze the larvae along the leaves. Sticky strands of silk from the larvae act like glue to hold the leaves together.

silk—long, thin threads that stick together to make a cocoon

larva—an insect at the stage of development between an egg and an adult; more than one larva is called larvae.

WHERE WEAVER ANTS LIVE

Weaver ants live in forest trees in hot places.

Baya Weavers

Male baya weavers use blades of grass and palm leaves to make their nests. The bird weaves the pieces together with its beak and claw. Then it adds a long **tunnel** to the nest. The bird uses the tunnel to enter its home. Predators cannot get inside.

tunnel—a narrow passageway

WHERE BAYA WEAVERS LIVE

Baya weavers build nests in trees. They look for branches that hang over water.

FACT

Males use their nests to attract mates.

Paper Wasps

Paper wasps make nests from chewed wood and **saliva**. The **queens** and other female wasps scrape off wood from trees and fence posts. They chew the wood and mix it with their saliva to make **pulp**. The wasps make **cells** in the nest. These spaces hold their eggs. The pulp turns into paper when it hardens and dries.

saliva—the liquid in the mouth

queen—an adult female wasp or other insect that lays eggs

pulp—a mixture of ground up paper and water

cell—a small space; one of the spaces in a paper wasp nest is a cell.

WHERE PAPER WASPS LIVE
Look in covered areas, such as under tree branches and porch ceilings.

RANGE MAP

Chimpanzees

After a long day, chimpanzees build nests high up in trees to sleep. They bend and weave long branches to make strong nests. Then they flatten the nests. Leaves and twigs make a soft mattress. Chimpanzees build their beds in only a few minutes!

FACT

Sleeping in trees helps keep chimpanzees safe from predators on the ground. Chimpanzees need strong nests so they don't fall to the ground.

Chimpanzees build nests high up in rain forests and woodlands in Africa.

RANGE MAP

21

Glossary

cell (SEL)—a small space; one of the spaces in a paper wasp nest is a cell.

domed (DOHMD)—rounded on top

larva (LAR-vuh)—an insect at the stage of development between an egg and an adult; more than one larva is called larvae.

offspring (OFF-spring)—the young of a person, animal, or plant

predator (PRED-uh-tur)—an animal that hunts other animals for food

pulp (PUHLP)—a mixture of ground up paper and water

queen (KWEEN)—an adult female wasp or other insect that lays eggs

saliva (suh-LYE-vuh)—the liquid in the mouth

silk (SILK)—long, thin threads that stick together to make a cocoon

sociable (SOH-shuhl-buhl)—tending to live in groups or packs

tunnel (TUHN-nuhl)—a narrow passageway

weave (WEEV)—to pass grass, sticks, and other materials over and under one another to make a nest

Read More

Danielson, Ethan. *Inside Bird Nests.* Inside Animal Homes. New York: PowerKids Press, 2016.

Garland, Michael. *Birds Make Nests.* New York: Holiday House, 2017.

Peterson, Megan Cooley. *Chimpanzees Are Awesome!* Awesome African Animals! North Mankato, Minn.: Capstone Press, 2015.

Internet Sites

Use FactHound to find Internet sites related to this book.

Visit *www.facthound.com*

Just type in 9781543526820 and go.

Check out projects, games, and lots more at
www.capstonekids.com

Avon Public Library

Critical Thinking Questions

1. Name three ways that birds and other animals keep predators away from their homes.

2. How does the sun help birds and insects when they're making their nests?

3. Why do some birds build their nests on branches that hang over water?

Index